*Angels the Size
of Houses*

Aaron Kent

Angels the Size of Houses

Shearsman Books

First published in the United Kingdom in 2021 by
Shearsman Books
PO Box 4239
Swindon
SN3 9FN

Shearsman Books Ltd Registered Office
30–31 St. James Place, Mangotsfield, Bristol BS16 9JB
(this address not for correspondence)

www.shearsman.com

ISBN 978-1-84861-766-7

ACKNOWLEDGEMENTS

I'd like to thank the editors of *Wild Court, Prototype, Prelude,* Crested Tit Collective (*Rewilding: An Ecopoetic Anthology*), Wild West Press (*One In All In* anthology), *Iamb*, and Dostoyevsky Wannabe (*The Rink*) where these poems originally appeared in varied, initial forms.

I'd also like to thank a variety of individuals who have made this possible. Emma Kennedy for her consistent belief in me. Rue Frances Scout Kennedy and Otis Jenő Fox Kennedy who do not know how important they were to this book, yet. Andrew McMillan, Gillian Clarke, Theophilius Kwek, and Jeremy Prynne for their support of this book. Tony Frazer for inspiring me as a publisher and as an editor. Jennifer Edgecombe and Charlie Baylis for having read these poems in various forms, at various stages. And Frances Leake, Elizabeth Kennedy, Jazmine Linklater, Jack Warren, Gurdeep Mattu, Suna Afshan, Dominic Leonard, Kate Rizzo, Stuart McPherson. Adrian B. Earle, Tom Snarsky, Martha Sprackland, and Matteo Morandi.

Contents

Vanilla / 9

Elements IV: Carpentry Exam / 11

A Black and White Photo of Bioluminescence / 13

Dear Mother You're Dying / 15

I Have Eaten the Moths and Now My Mouth Is Soot / 16

Life Is a Perpetual Trauma Machine / 17

Morning in Retrograde Part II / 18

Elements III: Sapin Noir / 19

The Perimeter of a Femur / 21

Portmanteau / 22

In the Span of Five Hours / 24

Musical Passages for Theatre Interludes / 25

Cress Soil / 26

Ice Skating, Garden of Eden, 1998 / 27

Levant 1919 – March to Ruin; Swollen Dead / 29

Iona / 31

Psykos*/*((Girlyas)) / 32

Moving My Family into a Den in the Corner of the House / 33

Ration As a Sum (Weight of / Our Stomach Lining) / 34

Contingency Plan: Red Circles (Ophelia) / 35

A Kaleidoscope of Butterflies / 36

What's One Death / 38

All Five Fingers But One / 39

Amnesty International Workers / 41

Elements I: The Sober Spirit / 41

Container Poem / A Space for Improvement / 43

The Mountain's Ugly Head / 44

Rise Balance Rise / 45

Blood Red Blister / 47

Reasons to Take Part in a Treasure Hunt / 49

Hail Sincerity / 50

Skidbladnir / 51

Morning in Retrograde Part I / 53

Elements II: Your Tree Is in Decay / 55

The Old Man, The Boats / 56

Snow Smear / 58

Northern Siberian Sign / 59

Yellow / Red / Cot / 60

The Reservoir / 62

Still Fires / 64

The Dead Love the Unborn / 66

Old Fisherman Kosztka / 68

Feralism 101 / 70

The Stress of Movement / 71

For Rue. For Otis.

Vanilla

Eighteen verses of birdsong
pull our boundaries towards
the heavens in a cynical display
of gesture and gesticulation.

> *Aaron*, the editor begs, *you cry angels*
> – the volatility of spirituality as prayer
> is evident – *then kiss the back of your neck*
> *as if in serendipitous loss.*

I've got low blood pressure
stamped into the pulse
of my temporal lobe where I feed
nightly seizures with rat poison

and an idiot's guide to night terrors:
don't scare the children,
eat dark chocolate,
be intrinsic in your grief.

If I can learn to drink gravity's lust,
it can split the vertigo I have wrapped
and assumed for the birth of my son.
His eyes; two oysters with tape radial

the pearls, the living dead with asthma
pumps, a catch of the mirror
in the dead of night. Otis was born
driven by Gods the size of houses

and armed with the luck of Ouija boards,
a smile entrenched in every nap
cut short by abrupt chaos. In my waking
I now dance in vanilla pods, salute

the sun's waning epaulets and pray
for the dead to wake in clusters
so we are pleasantly surprised in aftermath;
silent in broken stride. Rue, radical.

Otis, scientific. Emma lacing mastitis
through the bed / consumed by others.
My eyes; a mistake on a postmodern canvas,
two holes in a hot air balloon, watching angels

kiss the back of their necks.

Elements IV: Carpentry Exam

Dark in firefly histrionics
where sleep takes the shape of lightbulbs
oozing vagabond tricks
and *love the ocean, I love the ocean.*
Thematically you direct intention
to maintain eye contact,

a motif in precise movement,
yet we are two points in an ocean,
semblance in balanced resuscitation.
Two buoys separated
by a turn of the century
on the back-broken rem,

I called down to the shop to get coffee;
chewed the beans raw on the way back up;
you never stirred
as I caffeinated a volatile addiction.
We have both felt the arc
of narratives where our paths path,

we the rivers swell across the stage
and our convergence is no longer two elements
but a singular unanimous unison
of forward planning.
I promise to try to clean the hand
and we can bring ourselves into moments

where the crowd is in gentle song
for matrimony
in which we expect to be iridescent.

And angry.
But we, the scales, get heavier on one side
and we begin to push our feet

into terror, firm and low;
because we can kick our ancestors out,
deserted by his own daughter but not his own.
By the hysterics of rage
and the heavy-gloved hand
so as not to cleanse analogue radio

now dead alongside the memory
late cold dinner.
We are all to feed ourselves
but ourself is harder to work
more for less and the versus them:
it's about us, *versus us*,

versus a method where we can all find
to stop the drift of tender reasoning.

A Black and White Photo of Bioluminescence

The night's knot
    comes loose
with the gravitational pull
      of   lunar vessels.   The coil's heart
pumps depth charges
    the shape
of homesickness   – we wait
    like stolen children. Us.   Waiting.

We learnt algebra,   studied lines
    of broken expressions,
        the skull
and shape of the sum.   Pause
    in the crook
    of swollen sleep.
    There are languages   we share
    in Morse code   /   kilohertz.

    Twenty degrees
longitudinal.

We drift back   and forth   each hydrangea night
    on orbits
      we find mapped
      on the back
of receipts.
    No size or space
      captures the turn of rem.

Three tiny moons
    among Icarus'
      first flight,

two   splintered boats
across the face of Saturn.
                          Anthe
somewhere in the distance.

Dear Mother You're Dying

You are wasting away, you have
cavernous sinuses and hollow flesh.
Eat gracefully: there are those that are starving,
you told us this and shoved our faces into

Mother, ten years dead and veering further
right. We held a wake while you overslept,
I forgot your name, had to cycle through
every teacher I knew before I got Mother

you're like communal wine: a representation of
blood. This is how we love each other now,
posthumously, wafer thin, before a father who
believes in spirits more than us. I've tried to save

you, but you don't need saving – there are scars
on your pupils, lessons embedded in the corner,
rope knotted red in veins across your milk-
lapped eyeballs. Your funeral was joyous, we sung

the only song you ever knew. Your body so pale,
So sodden in drowning, you are course corrected,
Mother. You were as small and tight as a
lock of hair at birth. I've tried to shut the

casket but your arms stick to the seal. You've
been dead longer than you were living, Mother,
and we've left a hole next to yours. Two singing
bodies.

I Have Eaten The Moths
And Now My Mouth Is Soot

We are three bombs away from night time pressing
halos into the rear-view mirror. Why do you shake
when you bleed, when you scream, when we love?
I have cut the ties to my past life, and you are aware
of every mistake I made in transcribing my old notes
onto sheet music.

At first it was the size and shape of the bars, but we
later learnt that every house has a back door, and
every home has an emergency exit. To take away the
pride of an escape is to mute the scenarios in which
we find ourselves at our bravest. I have given myself
the darkest seeds.

I am still uncertain how to proceed with this tumour.
It eats at my soul, and I hear it rapping at the keyboard
when you can't sleep and the hypnotherapy has
deserted me. You are fresh in morning dew, and wearing
the same shapes I gave to that sweet, derelict, old
church we married in.

Life is a Perpetual Trauma Machine

It is essential we roll from tummy to back
before we learn to roll over in our graves.
There were frostbitten maps in the nursery
among footpaths to the back of winter.
My wife dreamt she threw a tantrum. She watched
our daughter's blood drain from her before
she woke to the air broken thin with a sweetness
of morning espresso. I told her I only dream
of Anthe and salt in both sea spray and road
markings. I bought a book in the art of rebellion
against the dynamics of traffic management:
'It is inevitable to be, to lose, the loss of lust
in lost linings in mapped markings.' We walk
two by two into verse and version of stigmatic
boat – the fondue – my blood plasma – and the neighbours
invited over to claim a stake in calamity.
When we docked on the shoreline I read the unicorn
skulls, dim light emitting enough indecision
to conquer your weight. In stolen fear of my sleep,
you found attraction both sweet and steep, sleep
as sleet in wartime. Again the trees are victims
this morning, we hear the crook of branches screaming
for an eternal wind; every inch of soil offered
a chance to salt our mat for Brahms in breastfed
luxury. Every day another rendition of a life
we failed to compose. Every day another rendition
of a life we compose after the fact. All of us pressed
evenly as broken paint on the nape of her neck,
and yours in the small hours. The tiniest hairs
match, we are jigsaw pieces for a greater portrait.
We walked two by two into a singular
morning and broke the night with perpetual concern.

Morning in Retrograde Part II

The mouse has left the doorstep, burnt grass and blackbird's wing. We have pruned the bougainvillea of aphids, left the thorns for new tenants to prick – bloody tongued and open mouthed. You are near with shattered tiara and a break in the fabric of our house, this calm wastrel we managed to conceive a family in. I will never clear the electric meter from my fisherman's chest, nor burden myself with the most efficient method of dispensing spirits. Play the stream once more, pluck the harp from our baby's head and grant me the serenity to build a new lawn away from the granite of a town built to hold a history.

Elements III: Sapin Noir

it is the lightest section of the
            courage of broken glass
as the nest is combined with propane
                hence swarming to the television with
                        everything our child sees in harvest
this biomass of mass of crawling in every direction
        but the entranced hornet's nest you clamber for
shrugged and omniscient in
        cross and touch and cliché led to
                different futures on the same
        surface so friction lends us a

burning to glory together therein
loss and the band plays funeral

uplifted by harmonium jewellery and
dressed coastal ships land where
                the water meets claw any space that
                belongs to anyone that isn't us
                and my grandfather has been

        bled though his flesh is charred
beer at three am five am seven am am dead
        blow dealt by politicians
                concussion from the rooftops of
working extra to pay the bills and
                working harder to work less for more
                and the others are working
                discrepancy isn't about us
                the right balance this is how i see

our sofa-surfing and our methods
the floor with all the force of return

The Perimeter of a Femur

In sores confirmed to be late romance
I have offered weeping platitudes at the funeral
of Whitman's poetry. The strange bruises
I have paid for in litigated circumstance

have been clutched from the back
of Satan's neck, and there is now
an interminable wait for rabidity

to blister bone and shard the core
of a coronary attack. We are all just salt
and sand; a mixture of the crow's
sharpened craw and a predatorial instinct
for the nothing of eventuality. *Be patient,*

I told my son, *for moonlight will eventually split
Saturn's rings, and you will again dream of Anthe
and every term I've used to describe you and your sister.*

Anthophobia wraps a bouquet of Begonia
in newspaper and leaves them on the doorstep
for asthma to caress. I wheeze pearls and daughters,
time as retreat from the snowcaps of distant planets.

I am pressed against tile, moisturised
and crying – waiting in pollen for the night
to stalactite infinity pools of dew. Lay me prone
and rigid, press one hand into my groin,
and clutch a thermometer as we prepare
the bedroom for my maceration.

Portmanteau

All of us; you, Aaron Kent, and I
spread ourselves across the mattress
where we read ergodic fiction to each other –
where she lay the golden chariot,
alchemy by alchemist,
unenviable task of poisoning
the dinner party. We bought a simile,
like we had bought a mouse –
petted, fed, hygienic
born to serve a different purpose.
We, all Aaron, carried him in our arms,
our wasted arms in nuclear unrest,
and dug lead into turf
as we pressed its aching body
into a shoebox and begged
each other for entropy. The tone
of conversation had changed
and the split had guaranteed doubt.
I've seen myself against a foreign backdrop
like the breast of a white swan
paralysed by the lines and ripples
elegantly stamped on water's canopy,
where the drinks are quaffed
before the bruschetta stuffed.
Three of us, the inheritance of each other,
like buds snatching for the sun,
sent to follow a slope so weak so long so dark
against the paleness that eats the very best
of every silver lining etched in the folds
of heavy cloth / case. I still hear them,
us, myself in every quaint out-dated

piano solo of a rehearsed broken
moonlight sonata, like a sober actor
playing drunk – the chimes jangling
somewhere in absentia,
the simile sleeping on the crook of midnight,
a desperation becoming faint. I overcame
and landed with tender spring
between the three of us
there, between the Godlessness of uncertainty.

In the Span of Five Hours

We've wrapped the horse in blessings
from the Arctic's snow-driven tide,
in tune with frequencies you and I
can only hear when you are perpendicular
to the wash of insulation and mist.
L'hippocampe is in our midst,
my heart is in the back of its throat
and you appreciate the gesture.

These lights are visitors we ignore
like the unwavering peculiarities
            of our trans-lingual futures.
I draw a straight line from hospital
corners, carrying a tape measure
and your stomach in centimetres.
Each notch is another day's wait
marked in kilohertz and graph paper.

I draw stethoscopes on heart monitors
and lean into the curtain to calm us.
We have the shimmer of youth
and the interruption of morning dew
to guide us back to our heavy home.
We tear through names as if burning
            the span of our wings.
And you think you like Lazarus.

Musical Passages for Theatre Interludes

I sing the rhythm-struck gauntlet,
the wax coated blade
on the west of my pupils.
From left-field a harp struck
with all edges of solar's
Plexus – a pair of brothers
in the diamond fields
picking coal. I turn the soil
in fresh adventure
and pasteurise tomorrow's
memories with seeds
from the grasslands.
I wear the weather as Marianna
Trench, all the cattle shown
to the front of the line,
remove the burns
from individual stems
and count the petals left
in a state of perpetual
infinity. Bliss picks the snow
from the tread and counts
the plug sockets in service
station bathrooms. I pick
the dead mites from my
dreams and sabotage leisure
time in my mother's
swollen axis.

Cress Soil

The moon doth shine as bright as day
once we lit the craters and made
arsonists of astronauts – this town keeps
its road-signs to itself – since the streets
were feinted gold to remind us how the
greatest Marxists are second or third
generation council estate kids; I kid
you, knot the ropes (are best shown
from distance as is the beauty of broken
noses and split lips) spilt ship break
waves goodbye too much too long for
the have nots and the must haves must
half the mast hand [on page thirteen
there is a paltry attempt at deception]
who sells them as black and white sweets.

Ice Skating, Garden of Eden, 1998

When the floods erred
over the pyre, the ice
caps were still ideas –
a convergence of crystal
starlings invoking themselves
to a hemisphere. My father
still spoke in Rather,
comparing potential
to outcome and living
through the theoretical
choices of a coin flip.
(Nothing would prepare
him for a side, a continuum
never considered ad
infinitum). In evening's
grubby light we married
mushroom while he sung
broken harmonica
for an orchestra of junction –
the tip forms; mistakes
we promised to make,
a space to take. You, I
was told when we
returned from the registry
office, sledded down
Wollaton hill in the first
stretch of snow; your first
instinct to battle and claim
each sheet like condensation
racing to the bottom,
engorging itself on itself. I piled

snow against the door of a man
you never met, a cleansed
soul burdened with a front
he couldn't forecast. The cat
determined to hide in his arms,
the whistle of his harmonica
drowned out by a meow
stretched thin across the
enveloping mist. I broke
my arms in a race to the finish,
I snapped my tendons
to calm the light.

Levant 1919 – March to Ruin;
Swollen Dead

Other materials, even in iron
pressed fatigue. The calm
precedes the storm precedes sleep
stretched so thin it is broken
in twilight. Home is void by work,
miners are void by pattern.

Full of intent, patterns
of populace against iron
for the sake of cheap work.
Cracks spread across calm
chatter, the bulk of broken
beams turn'd loose in sleep,

so deep to be eternal sleep.
Every timber leaves a pattern
neither confirmed nor broken
 in the wake of the iron.
There is a permanent calm
with the permanent loss of work.

Choked by the need for work
in the palm of dead; sleep
as insurance against calm
infinity. the depth of patterns
in the onyx of an iron
wall. The rods are made to be broken

and rebuilt to be broken
again. Across the soiled work

tundra, run beneath iron
rain scalding the dreams; sleep
tonight in delicate pupils. Pattern
patchwork fields for the rest, calm

to be laid upon the sweet, calm
soil. Tin prices are made to be broken
and lost as prayers spread pattern
across a duchy sky. The end of work
and the frightful, long sleep
of an anxious walk to ruin. Iron

every calm friend lost to work
into all of the night's broken sleep.
Press their pattern deep with iron.

Iona

We could move
>to the isle of Iona

and paint horses
>with our left hands

completely blindfolded
>before the canvas

you could talk
>to the birds

and be their jewels
>heaven sent

and glitter prone
>while I grow

a branch
>from my belly button

and let it pierce
>the walls

of our house

Psykos*/*((Girlyas))

I'm alone on the western front,
again,

I'm handcuffed to the shore
and I launch myself into
work. It won't

be long, gunslinger, won't be
years before the minotaur chorus
[we're the chorus, the slender

minotaur]
wounds.   You w/o me & us converging
                                 let us speak, let us, let us, let
                                 us

speak plot.
Peninsula, you're cap smoke to the
right temple, it's early

easy morning. Operator, we only
phone the wrong numbers. My
daughter speaks in keys

now and she ain't & she is. And
you ain't. You certainly ain't.

Moving My Family into a Den
in the Corner of the House

We are the by-product of every wasted binliner.
    It is in these sacks that I want to find you, redemption.
I have built, buildings, built a den, den, den in the back

    of my hand read like a fortune teller. We, you and I,
husband and wife, should carry our daughter safely,
    so not to bang her skull and make halos the size of

houses. The atom has been split and I am waiting for
    it to whisper my name in the sweet embrace of dusk.
It is there we can cower less, coward less, courage

    lest the spiders eat our souls. Yours first, then mine,
mine a peach pit, mine a mine, yours the crumb from
    a chocolate cake. Our daughter's too fresh to fully

understand the difference between a soul set aside
    for the ripening and nuclear devastation.

Ration As a Sum
(Weight of / Our Stomach Lining)

Invest in news articles,
articulate hunger as a sign of everything
that has been painted onto the back of seedy bars.

Wear halos to dinner parties.

The beans have been torn open,
we are bleeding from our palms.

We have read all the psalms
and found them wanting,
where is Christ in a house like this?

The square footage is almost funny,
if it weren't for the fallout,
the arguing,
the radiation.

Planet Earth has given us back our days
in exchange for vouchers.

Two for one on Laundromat remnants,
and a discount on the cost of neighbourly conversation.

It is hard to keep up the premise that we are a nuclear family
when the water bearers aren't sure if they are lion
or crab or neither.

We think there are still constellations.

We strain our necks to look.

Contingency Plan: Red Circles (Ophelia)

Ivory sinks the plum's flesh into the gate
    of heaven, weakness is present in every
  inch of the cheek. She has a foxes cry
    and crime to frost in the parlour, we
never call it the parlour, but I do ask parlez-vouz
  Français? Her tongue is undone by a run
of weak spots and sun spots in antithesis of
    dialogue, and it's no wonder
she truly speaks fox. The weight of heirlooms
  we can never offer because we can
never offer, because we can never stop
    collecting junk in the hope it means
    something. I am holding her first tooth
and you are present with anaesthetic.

A Kaleidoscope of Butterflies

These clipboards are just pictures
of home falling on a bubble,
furniture we tested in Ikea

while simulating resplendence.
Every calm grace whispered
as prayer needs a deity

desperate to listen in,
a paranoid voice rejoice
invasion. The softness of us

like bruised peaches covered
in the honeyed mould of
intent – an invitation

to thumb and cajole.
I chose anything yellow,
anything like turning

a light on. Our life has
accumulated more beginnings
than ends and you have

panchromatic eyes while
I live in blue greens. Range
testing, sound navigation,

long shots in short spurts.
Deep devilled eyes
like woodpecker alarms,

each second cry is a sweet
serendipitous irony
tickling the chin of wolves.

We are torn either side
of the coffee table,
positioned among abrupt

chaos and a gentle cavalcade.
When I watch them watch
us I hear the tender swell,

polishing their stomachs
so they can better eat us,
our fresh repetitions, and

skin the bones for a new
beginning again. A new
beginning. Again.

What's One Death

I had seen his bedside manner

More often than not, and learnt
How he crashed into bed like

A lighthouse batters the ocean
In glare. Their howls phonetic

In the sustenance of each other,
A canopy between them of

Linen and lint. He would wake
With the appetite of a wolf,

Creep into the Rayburn-warmed
Kitchen, and murder a cub for

its voice, to cry for a fuller moon.

All Five Fingers But One

Your tears are a tear
in the space-time fabric,
there are two moons
textiled across the sky
and I build bridges
to houses that never exist.

The ocean cries on my doorstep.
I knock. I knock.
Twice for no.
We blossom halos
in the atmosphere
across from the sewing machine,

and you, broken
you, you eat the first fruit
of the harvest before sleep
settles. We can never see the fields,
patchwork and patched,
hay woven into buildings. You.

Built. Two hands, to weave,
two hands hung to- dry in tears
and saline solutions.
We feed on mulberries, pick
turpentine eventualities
from deciduous trees

growing in the wardrobe.
There are books to burn.
There are never enough books

to burn through
on these cold nights.
I shed my skin first

so you can see
I am polished bone
and stretched muscle.
You leave your soul
behind
for battening.

Amnesty International Workers
[Campaign for Nuclear Disarmament]

The night has calmed to the point we can't process
our features in the dark room.

Everything is no longer a dark room.

You have told our daughter to cover her eyes so
often I worry she will forget how to open them
when the dreams start.

I have wasted our halos on an argument against
the inevitable.

Dangerous men become more powerful
with every act.

Every act more powerful with every man.

Every man a temper tantrum away from us.

We remain at the edges, waiting to be excused.

We forget we are working class / We are disposable.

Elements I: The Sober Spirit

it is the smallest
        cherry blossom
    that halts traffic
while the world does not stop
            to count the coyotes
      piled up on the side
of the road
      waiting for their ship to come in

I've always believed

         if you stare too long
          at the dead
       their eyes blink
    and acknowledge an afterlife
   where dreams are read from unicorn skulls
and we are all born under lucky stars

    the white rose is a symbol
    just like a stop sign is a symbol
    of every mistake that lead to its erection

Container Poem /
A Space for Improvement

My hypnotherapist tells me
sharks chase **nuclear bombs**
when we watch the news
too much, and I press the
        trigger.

I have given her all of the
planets in tiny **rubber marble**
form, all of them except Earth
which I need if I'm to ever visit
        Italy.

The Mountain's Ugly Head

The bark opens the bite of Russia.
      Two marks thumbed into
      providence, bled dry under her
      palliative snowfall.
      Idless Valley waits for
      Aspen, counts the blind
      static for heaven's form.

Three Russian lunar cycles design
      the syllabic structure,
      how the tongue rolls
      the digraph against
      saponification's rub.
      Proper pronunciation
      requires the national

accent.

Rise Balance Rise

Finally the tree came down
for cast and termination.
In the end it was a game
of chess, in the end everything
is. The trick is in the knowing.
I brought the bends, moved
diagonally like a missile
beached on a tattoo of
a mandala – the sky hanged
fresh like linen. I swaddled
the Swedish pine, took
the sander to our palms.
Together we approached
pharmacy corridors like
we hadn't found the splinters,
like a flamingo learns to balance
or risk perpetual motion.
When you sink you wonder
how much difference a synonym
makes – how much drowning
is just an end to sinking
in the same way suffocation
is an end to sleeping late
and coffee early. The act
requires the trick. We had
equations on our hands,
sight lines of the final
act: the spectacle of destruction
screaming 'timber' like
screaming 'flesh' at a funeral.
Heavier than the weight

of footsteps, lighter than
root and a branch.

Blood Red Blister

As if veering towards the bottom
of the stretchmarks – in tender
climates and tepid amusement –
macchiato spilt on moustache

and unprepared to hold muslin.
First born and weighed from
branches, golden toothed in interrupted
sleep. Even outer Hebrides split

apart don't mount the red bloom
of debut kisses. Lathered in spring
and cherried in terminal baths, wretched
in palpitations. The caffeine of silence

is enough to turn love's hand towards
a void. A tongue on the roof of the fly's
mouth, damp and concerned with
the ephemera of lamps. Wedded

to the weakest bridge, unpaid
but for the paint's chip. Lost in anchor,
feet firmed to the swollen bubbles of last night –
dinner plates. A patch of stubble

holding flecks of ginger, in dead
of night prayers to be awoken.
Persimmon fruits in the back
of the store, shrouded in Irish

folklore and a missing girl's
storytelling. The broken ears perch
for a new rug to ignite. The squeezing
sensation in index, for the gloss

to push impossible. A barista as missionary,
working through the pain of a hangnail
and a missed lunch break at noon on Tuesday.

Reasons to Take Part in a Treasure Hunt

Time consumption is mindlessness,
    you are the waste of water,
        there are stars in the back rooms of your neighbour's houses

    how will you ever know about them if you don't search?

The cats tell us how to move,
    the world is shaped like an egg,
        every part of your face tells a lie you tried to keep,

    I have eaten both of your novels; neither tasted like paper.

Your sanity has fallen into the wrong hands,
    your mouth is open too wide for your feet,
        there are more ostriches than mistakes,

    you don't know to use a full stop.

Properly. If at all
    there is a no better time than the present tense,
        Kanye West is waiting,

    the whole town is waiting,

why do you keep us waiting?
    Just find it already.
The clues are there.

Hail Sincerity

In gentle aftermath
we find her pressed
against the edge,
and consequence,
of infirmity.
Both shoes tied
in umbilical knots
and a firm crown
of splintered marble.
You'll carry her
to the ocean's call
and I'll bring her
to Valhalla
and bathe her
in warrior's steel.

Skidbladnir

You lie in grids
    searching for Ilyria,
    laying your body
pāhoehoe across

the fan-driven wind.
    In later seasons
    uterine plexus
will whistle harp's edge

across the face of
    the freshly sunk snow.
    You pick the orange peel
from the Earth's crust

and lay waste to ideas
    about jogging.
    It is in prazosin headaches
I will learn to keep hold

of our elephant. All
    four tonnes
    of anticipation,
networks of cloth ready for bile.

I build routes to the bath
    and clean the top
    of the shelves
while you, blissful and unaware,

smile through your dreams.
    As if lost in the
    thoughts of our puppy.
As if chasing a last parade.

    As if everywhere not yet in bloom.

Morning in Retrograde Part I

I'll see you on the other side
of the moon, the grassy
knoll perched atop heaven's
chrysalis. In mist the fist
of the first leaves like pulling
a hand from the grave,
a-bomb flesh smattered
across petal-strewn bedroom
urn. I can cremate our friends
if you need a sacrifice.
Mozzarella torn fog people,
they want us for our teeth;
for a tooth: a single semibreve
from a full head of hair.
Night has burnt us once
again, dark chocolate weak
like melatonin streak popping
three – threeeeethreeeeethreeeee –
to sleep a dream of James Last
playing the river's mouth
with a flood of starlings. You
ask why poets write so often
of the moon – It's the consistency
of its change, the monthly
reveal of itself; waxing so
it can wane, a friend near
with knife. Knives. Two
fingers on steel morning.
We have disturbed our
child in nocturna, all
our pavor is just a scent.

The neighbours have smoked
our paint fumes, intoxicated
baby blue chipped memory.
The ceremony asks for torn hay
with broken crowns. We have outgrown
our roots, and now we
return to a home overgrown
with bougainvillea.

Elements II: Your Tree Is in Decay

You can sleep   at my house
        martyred minister,
you are more welcome than
        the clock   it
keeps us awake in passing
        resemblance to   a
child you   lost in the
        river Styx

Your   tall   thick   pine
        tree waits
on Bongraesan   I wish to
        be concealed in
gold acacia   sweet legumes
        burnt   pyre upon
the border between south
        and their   north

You have both halves with oxen
        in tension   violin
orchestral   moonlight plays
        a sonata bring all six.

The Old Man, The Boats

I'd rather be the fish than the fisherman.
The loaded sky, two barrels into a fever
dream, spitting teeth at the bedroom
window. I only know the rain from the
TAKK takking on the monitor, my daughter
face down in rested abandonment - the glint
of adventure something translucent
in the space between her and the ceiling.
Archimedes is the first answer
on the submariner's exam. TAKK.
Those weighted principles of sound
dispersal lean heavier underwater:
the doppler effect a protest song,
cavitation a calculation's difference
between a Russian sub and an
orchestra of shrimp. The ear learns
the difference between a fisherman's
prayers and the swaddle of the net
he drowns in. TAKK like thumbtack
like the titans sit in delirium swatting
radar, ushering along the afternoon.
Critiquing Hemingway is easier
than dreaming of sound, navigation,
ranging - our Bible a hand-carved
list of every vessel sleeping without
a dummy, each gargantuan star
level with bioluminescence. When you
count TAKK as recurring leaps
into love, you do so with the mouth
of somebody less bitten, less torn
by hook and battering ram. Tell
me if an anchor set thirty KLIKK is the

same as two tugs and a promise. Tell
me if I'm honest, humming nuclear way
three bunks deep in morning confidence.
This is a goodbye to harms way. A farewell
to arms, two limbs dangling limp
on limp. The most disappointed I've been
in water since watching a failed baptism
in the Atlantic, a single wave and welcome.
The rain TAKK, the flood TAKK, myself TAKK
at sunrise watching for signs of drowning.

Snow Smear

You and I – spread – wafer thin
        across hollow prism needles,
I love you with low visibility,
a pack of thermal gloves, and

glow sticks. The banks are lit up
like bioluminescence at a wedding
        or that baby bump glow
before the life change, here we

melt in time; torn I quit bleeding
so springtails may replace my
nervous system with an itch
        so splendid it causes

        us to tear off my skin
and cook it on the campfire. You
see, *this* is love: us, eating my
flesh under platelet dark clouds.

Northern Siberian Sign

Building a heartbeat has brought
myxomatosis to the doorstep,
swollen plump on bottled stress
pecked deep/weak in morning's
inarguable bliss. All years shine
throughout you – and I love you

the same way I tie my shoelaces
as bunny ears born altricial fresh
along the northern fault line
of my depth perception. I see
your shoes and know you are
criss-crossed. 'Rice cakes made

by rabbits on the moon.' This
is how I know we are married,
when we hold hands and kiss
deep in the throes of blindness,
fever, and fatigue – before the
tumours inevitably set in.

Yellow / Red / Cot

The flesh is in the angle shape and angle
    of both instances where apt and incapable
    of change for wait the snow is weak
I too both degrees in error we are yet to voice concerns
multiple fragilities under ice
    you have the best of both worlds
    calming presence in juxtaposition of night
wait for heavy set sleep sweet & steep

minutes of stress load-bearing birds tapping
    in frantic measures icebergs
    two for the way we dress ourselves
calming calling a place to return to in the small
crevices found into the wait of both carriages
    for the night's loss you have both
    I consider one at a time the voice when raised
is lost it is too soon for crawling I can hear her

calling the bees from oblivion the voice in hollow
    harrowing stance broken stanzas
    in the shape of sums we calculated on
restaurant napkins the axis of both parts
pressed into third angle loss in left turn
    flood water broken height stones
    the size of angels the size of houses
frantic speech allows for the waste weight

shaped in severance calm now placement
    our blanket away from infinity
    the mist has swollen under the beak of kitchen tables
a tableau of investigations swollen sum there is no dream

just patient arousal of nature nurture is
    a violent nutritional waste keep talking
    weighted voice carpentry mistakes in
effervescence light is lost in you and our memories

in boxes clean white shoes and late fathers
    be late and brave and the sum of every
    part head north avenue in suite of Bach series
of notes on lined paper written twice struck through
golden waste intervals the streets are ice and flood
    this line lone alone in aisles I'll pick up halos
    across from the textile shelves for bouquets of
glitter not my favourite conscience time the flight of stairs

to the second reason compass as angled heat
    hold   face   turn from the cot
    we are trying against the rain there
in the background two bells three learning
to hold noise in science articulate the sheets are
    melting under us as tears in the fabric
    of space tears spaced across fabric angled
climbing vines to clouds yours is the red balloon

mine yellow

The Reservoir

Raymond Road

We wore goalposts, moved through
grass like hayfever had rested in the pores
of our skin, buried itself like two centuries
of social inequality. You were going to
die young, a father of a toddler, your
backwards, pitted heart too heavy to
pump a whole life through. They taught

us to learn a trade, to unclog their shit
or rewire their house – so we could value
ourselves by how much they valued
our labour. You were a semi-detached
chav, I was terraced scum, the suffocation
of an estate still squeezed the core of us.
Your being was a furry apple, too long

in the bowl to be eaten, too fresh to be
thrown away. Allergic to the sight of
a countdown, your death set me sneezing
before I hit puberty, after the first surgery
I remember – clad black and white with
a whistle calling for medics. I saw you
blink the first raindrop away, the insurance

your father bought with high standing, that
flood held back at the door by the fence
he had rigged for the governors. I didn't feel
the Earth move, nor the pollen rapture
my wastebasket sinuses, but you knew
labour is replaceable, and every kid grows
to be torn apart by the thing that turns their

soul. The wall caved in, the posts brought
down, the trees wrestled in waterlog. I learnt
community is not the measure of an effort
to coordinate flora, it's the outpouring when
the banks open wide and the sky dips low
and we watch our best efforts float away on
a boat with a hole too big to hold a heart.

Still Fires

we had an earthquake
low magnitude murmuration
of our furniture
flocking to center stage
and our mothers ring
behind the peeled skirting
like an envelope licked dry

my father watched Blair mourn
Diana never cared for the ring
his knuckles swollen from
knocking on doors another
debt for the electric laced
the birthday cake with acid

tripping on loose wires
my mother pulling up the wood
we grappled with each
other fists on soft
flesh kneaded for spillages
and small adventures

we saw the cops as threat
to our domain every
ballet shut down with phone
ring evidence of our ability
to communicate with nature
and toy with heavens

our mother dug for it cursed
the gods that dispersed her love
grabbed us two by one
to dent skull firm press

the carpets shafts showed
us how old the tables were
our blemishes told us
how old we could be
a bruise betrayed a ring
sized for someone else

The Dead Love the Unborn

my father believes it was an
inside job; the way you loved me
when you met me; the same way
a qillin caresses the grass
unbowed;

wind chimes on the musk of
antlers; he was certain
it was a setup; a trap; conspiring
to show the rivets of his love;
among

the dots of each of his knuckles;
the conspiracy he explained
exists to keep me ignorant;
blinded by murmurations of
intensity

hammering at my bread basket;
keeping me satiated; like
children full of want; not
stained with lack; milk drunk;
sparkling;

the trick is to listen to the
moon telling us we are
doomed; not the government;
nor my wife; the poets don't
understand;

let him understand for me;
every job is an inside job;
he's right; but not in the way
he thinks; I whisper to you sat
inside

my heart; cuddling the crops
decimated by ravens;
bringing trinkets home through
crossed wires and beard
shavings.

Old Fisherman Kosztka

Long legged prey, tubular mover
besides me, grief-stricken me,
driving two fingers to the wind
away from post-romantic posturing.

Bambi galloping grieving silence,
I am weeping too loud for deer,
again. I am audible over the rain
chirping like crickets on the windscreen.

Fricative fawn, sun flares and flora.
Today I learnt I am concurrent,
diminutive in respect of Saturn,
wire strung sharp by roving fauna.

When my mother phones I ignore
it. Its never her, always some bank,
but I've made my phone tell me
every call is an expression of her loss.

Pre-deer, pre-spotted wind, we sat
like ships in the night, port to port,
and pretended, for a moment, that
I stood a chance at redemption.

Two-toned vehicle, grief machine
in motion. We are whole together,
separate together, tone-deaf
for symmetry. One day my mother

will really call and I'll thank her
for the information, tell her I'm not
interested in a loan. I had one,
once, and I'm still paying it back.

Feralism 101

In the event horizon of a cull,
they'll paint us black and white
leach us across tuberculosis'

sympathetic face. Set like milk
marked wide from eye to eye,
they'll coax us feverish within

the soil, bludgeon the fat
reserves from our winter sleep.
They won't let us flea least concern

that we are; enviable scavenge
dig the home we love, sleep
rob the rain pitter pattered worms.

We do not spread neat on bone
ash like cattle, tyre torn salt
lick speed bump, intestines

worked over the face of an
open moon. We are cete heavy
in foddered abundance.

The Stress of Movement

The hemispheres you traverse are split
like fresh grapefruit on the breakfast table,
forming perpetual energy
and something of a vacuum.
That's the problem,
isn't it,

that living requires the futility
of continuance
against the blue-stamped topography
of peaks and troughs
that define our medications
and our polar shifts

in love. It is weighted against
my capillaries
that when you speak of blood,
the tender red reason
to share a birthday,
you speak of me.

This carries us across the Tamar,
beyond the valleys
and here into the heart of *us*,
clenched tight as a balled fist
awaiting the first signs
of blackbirds at dawn.

Lightning Source UK Ltd.
Milton Keynes UK
UKHW010023100721
386911UK00001B/61